For:

Toni Bowen

From:

Celia Heaton

Date:

5-9-03

Thanks for always being
there!

Gifts
from my
Front Porch

Inspirational Thoughts, Insights, & Reflections

THE
POPULAR
GROUP

New York, New York

Gifts from My Front Porch
ISBN 1-59027-041-X

Copyright © 2002 by GRQ Ink, Inc.
1948 Green Hills Boulevard
Franklin, Tennessee 37067

Published by **Popular Publishing** Company, LLC
3 Park Avenue
New York, New York 10016

Developed by GRQ Ink, Inc.
Cover design, interior design, and composition
by Whisner Design Group, Tulsa, Oklahoma

Illustrations by Taylor Bruce, Geyersville, California

From My Front Porch

It's dawn on a summer morning. I am sitting quietly in my rocker on the front porch, my hands cupped around a steaming cup of coffee. The birds are waking up—stillness.

My neighbors are still asleep. As I look up and down the street, I realize that each quiet house has its own story to tell. One of my neighbors is coping with unemployment. Down the street, another neighbor is planning a backyard wedding for her daughter. Next door, a single mom is struggling with the ravages of divorce.

I whisper a prayer for all those who live in my neighborhood. I know that God can also see them from His own front porch. "Bless them Lord with truth, joy, and prosperity," I pray. "Bless them."

For God so loved the world,
that he gave his only begotten Son,
that whosoever believeth in him should
not perish, but have everlasting life.

JOHN 3:16 KJV

——✠——

O God, I rejoice to give You
thanks and praise
for Your love for my neighborhood.
Amen.

My Neighbors

I find that my neighborhood is a wonderful place to practice God's love—but it's not easy. If you have lived in one place for long, it's likely that at least one of your neighbors has had an opportunity to rub you the wrong way.

I have a practice of praying for all my neighbors every morning. I pray that God will protect and defend each one from harm. However, recently a neighbor accused me of something I didn't do. And he didn't believe me when I told him I was innocent of the charge. I was furious.

And then, God showed me my error. I am to love my neighbors as I love myself—even when they behave badly. It reminds me that God's love is never deserved. It is a gift.

"Honor your father and your mother,"
and, "You shall love your
neighbor as yourself."

MATTHEW 19:19 NKJV

———〰———

God, I know that I don't always love my neighbors as
myself. Show me how to love my neighbors
and myself a little bit more today.

Amen.

A Gentle Rocking

The workday goes by so fast. I wake up before dawn, grab a cup of coffee, and race off to the office. At work, I'm running constantly between meetings, picking up voice mail, returning calls, reading, and responding to e-mail, trying to get some work done before the next meeting. At the end of the day, I rush home. God can get lost in all of that.

How sweet it is to sit on my front porch and rock gently back and forth. Slowly, slowly my senses reawaken to the presence of God. And I know, again, that I am always held tenderly in His arms.

You are He who took Me out
of the womb;
You make Me trust while on
My mother's breasts.

PSALM 22:9 NKJV

Slow me down, O God, and ease my mind.
Let me sit here and rock awhile with
You, quietly, slowly.

Amen.

Day's End

It's late but I can't sleep, so I slip out the front door to sit on the porch steps. All the houses on my street are dark and quiet. Only the sound of crickets breaks the silence.·

Inside my head, thoughts spin wildly. First I replay scenes from the day—various encounters with colleagues at the office, a phone call to a friend, playtime with the cats. Then my thoughts begin to slow as the dark quiet of the night descends upon me. And from somewhere deep inside, I hear a promise—"My peace I give to you." Peace. I sit for a long time, enjoying the peace of God.

My eyes are awake before each
watch of the night,
that I may meditate on your
promise.

Psalm 119:148 nrsv

———⟫⟫———

God, I cannot sleep tonight.
Calm my whirling mind and
let me focus on Your promise
to love me and grant me peace.
Amen.

The Wonder of Sparrows

I am a worrywart. I worry about work. I worry about my family. I worry about my home. I worry about money. I know that worry causes unnecessary fear, anxiety, and stress. I know this, yet I worry anyway.

But I also know how to get relief from all of my worries. I go out on my front porch and watch the birds bathing in the birdbath. They are so small, so vulnerable. Yet they splash and chirp and dry their feathers in the sunshine as if they have not a care in the world. As I sit and watch, my worry-weary mind remembers that the Bible says God takes care of the birds. If God takes care of the birds, then why should I worry? He will also take care of me.

The very hairs of your head are all numbered. Do not fear therefore; you are of more value than many sparrows.

LUKE 12:7 NKJV

O God, I am worried by
so many important
and unimportant
things. Help me to
learn from the birds today
how much You love me.
Amen.

Picking Up the Good News

I can always use a little good news. On Wednesdays and Fridays, I come home from work to find the neighborhood newspaper on my front porch. I live in a city that has long been plagued by crime, poor schools, and, for many of its citizens, poverty. But now we have a new mayor who is working hard to make the city a better place. My neighborhood paper reports that crime is down and more people are working than ever before. Hope has returned.

I used to think about moving to get away from the city's problems. Now, all this good news fills me with hope, and I want to stay and help make my city an even better place to live.

But there's more Good News. God loves me. And God loves my neighbors. God's love can change everything—even a city.

Bright eyes gladden the heart;
Good news puts fat on the bones.

PROVERBS 15:30 NAS

—◦—

Lord God, Your love changes everything.
Help me to take this Good News to the
neighbors I know and the neighbors
I have yet to meet.

Amen.

At Prayer on My Porch

My front porch is the perfect place for prayer. It's a quiet place where I can slip away from the demands of the day and talk with God for a little while. It offers me an opportunity to escape and enjoy God.

Sometimes on weekend afternoons, I sit in my rocker on the porch and pray with my eyes wide open. As I watch joggers running down my street, people taking a walk, or cars driving by, I say a little prayer for each one who passes my porch. I pray for neighbors at work in their front yards. Praying for neighbors, even strangers, somehow connects me to this place, my home. Prayer on the front porch helps me to remember that God watches over us all.

Now, O my God, I pray, let
Your eyes be open and
Your ears attentive to the
prayer offered in this place.

2 CHRONICLES 6:40 NAS

—⌇—

O God, let each one who passes
my front porch find peace.
Let each one know
Your love and care.
Amen.

A Prayer for the Front Door

Some Jewish families attach a mezuzah to the doorpost of their homes. The mezuzah contains a blessing for those who enter or a verse to remind the family of their faith.

While I don't have a mezuzah near my front door, I cover my front door in blessings and prayers for all those who enter. Here are a few of the prayers and blessings that adorn my front door:

"May all who enter here find God's peace."

"Bidden or not bidden, God is present."

"May you find in this place the open arms of Christ."

"May Your mercy, O God, cover all who come here."

The LORD bless you,
and keep you;
The LORD make His face
shine on you,
And be gracious to you;
The LORD lift up His
countenance on you,
And give you peace.

NUMBERS 6:24-26 NAS

—⁓—

O God, may everyone who
enters my front door
experience Your welcome
and Your joy.
Amen.

The Welcoming Voice

I enjoy living alone in my big house with its beautiful front porch. Well, I don't quite live alone—I have three cat companions. I once thought cats were quiet, solitary creatures, but I was wrong. When I come home from work, Sparky (the most vocal of the three) hears my car drive up. As I climb the porch steps and put my key into the lock, I hear the familiar moaning and groaning and whining of Sparky's "welcome home." No matter how stressful or difficult my day has been, Sparky's noisy welcome delights me.

When I get to Heaven, I believe God's angels will usher me into the presence of the King, and I will hear His voice welcome me to my heavenly home forever. What a wonderful day that will be!

The sound of the wings of the cherubim could be heard as far away as the outer court, like the voice of God Almighty when he speaks.

EZEKIEL 10:5 NIV

Let me hear Your welcoming
voice this day,
O God—a little bit of
Heaven in my world.
Amen.

Welcome

Be Still and Know

There's so much to do around the house. There are the two upstairs bedrooms to paint, the garden needs to be weeded, three loads of laundry wait patiently, the gutters must be cleared of leaves, and I haven't vacuumed in two weeks.

My front porch invites me to put off the chores a little bit longer. The world won't end because I have gutters to clear. I ease gratefully into the rocker on the porch and listen to the wind chimes singing softly in the breeze. The air is perfumed with the scent of jasmine growing over the porch. As I sit rocking gently, I hear God's voice deep within my heart—"There is time for everything. Be still and listen. I will tell you of My great love for you."

Be still, and know that I
am God;
I will be exalted among
the nations,
I will be exalted in the earth.

PSALM 46:10 NIV

———

O God, help me to be still and know Your love.
Amen.

God's Peace on This Place

I have a quote from a book by Thomas Merton in my cubicle at work. The quote is about Merton's longing to return to "Paradise," the place where he can recover his true identity and feel most completely himself. Merton was a monk living in a monastery. When he wrote about his "Paradise," he was referring to the solitude he enjoyed in a small hut in the woods nearby. My "Paradise" is the peace I seek when I return home every day after work.

When the Bible mentions "peace," it means much more than a sense of calm. It refers to a sense of utter wellness. When I sit on my front porch, I find "Paradise," God's healing peace.

*Peace, peace, to the far
and the near,
says the L*ORD*;
and I will heal them.*

ISAIAH 57:19 NRSV

———

O God, one thing I ask
above all others—today let
me find my "Paradise,"
let me know
Your healing peace.

Amen.

Knock

A knock on the front door alerts me that someone is standing on my front porch. When I open the door, I'm usually pleasantly surprised to find one of my friends or neighbors standing there.

I believe God is pleasantly surprised when we knock on His door with our prayers. In fact, I think God listens at the door, waiting for us to knock. He is always there, ready to answer. All we have to do is knock.

*Ask, and it shall be given you; seek,
and ye shall find; knock, and it shall
be opened unto you.*

MATTHEW 7:7 KJV

Behold, O God, I stand at the door and knock.
Let me know that You take pleasure
as we talk together.

Amen.

Peace to All Who Enter Here

Sometimes my world seems to be filled with war and peace at the same time. At work, the law of the jungle often prevails—only the strong survive. Road rage has made our freeways even more dangerous. A simple shopping trip to the mall bombards my senses with signs, bright lights, and loud, mindless jingles.

But God's peace can be found—even shared. When I fix dinner for friends or entertain neighbors on my front porch, there is always enough of God's peace to go around. We all find a refuge from the confusion and conflict of the day. Thank You, God, for giving me peace in the midst of the storm.

You shall say, "Have a long
life, peace be to you, and peace
be to your house, and peace be
to all that you have."

1 Samuel 25:6 nas

※

O God, let all who
enter my front door find
Your peace in the
hospitality I offer.
Amen.

Go with God

Long ago, family and guests were sent out into the world with a blessing. Often the blessing bestowed God's protection on those leaving home.

I have often wondered what became of this wonderful practice. When family and guests leave my front door, they step off my front porch into a world where anything can happen. Before they go, I ask God to bless them, to send His angels to protect them and watch over them.

"Go with God," I pray. "May God be with you wherever you travel. And may all God's angels defend you and keep you."

I hereby command you: Be strong and courageous; do not be frightened or dismayed, for the LORD your God is with you wherever you go.

JOSHUA 1:9 NRSV

—⟋⟍—

May Your protection and guidance,
O God, go with all who
leave my home.
Amen.

Coming Home

My cats are strictly indoor cats. They're also sneaky. One day when I answered a knock at the front door, Sparky shot out, crossed the street, and disappeared. I searched the neighborhood, calling his name, but there was no sign of Sparky. I was worried, upset, and angry.

In the early hours of the next morning, I was awakened by a pathetic yowling. Opening the front door, I found Sparky sitting on the porch crying to be let in. His ear was torn and bloody—but he was all right. I scooped him up. All my angry, worried thoughts disappeared as I hugged him.

Later, I thought, *If I feel such concern for a lost, skinny cat, how much more does God feel concern for me when I wander away from the safety of His presence?*

So he got up and went to his father. But while he was still a long way off, his father saw him and was filled with compassion for him; he ran to his son, threw his arms around him and kissed him.

Luke 15:20 niv

O God, Your love runs to greet me while
I am still far off. All praise to You!

Amen.

The Porch Light

I am afraid of the dark. That may seem like a strange admission, but the night frightens me. I don't like going out after dark, but I do—I must.

My return home is particularly uncomfortable until I see my porch light shining through the night, illuminating the path to my front door. My porch light reminds me that God is the Lord of my nights as well as my days. It helps me remember that God is always waiting to lead me home.

It's a simple thing, my porch light. But its warmth and welcome are a powerful sign of God's guidance and care.

The LORD went in front of them in a pillar of cloud by day, to lead them along the way, and in a pillar of fire by night, to give them light, so that they might travel by day and by night.

EXODUS 13:21 NRSV

Night has fallen, O God, and I turn to You for guidance and direction. Lead me to Your love, I pray.

Amen.

For Everything There Is a Season

I sit in my rocker in the spring and watch the magnolia tree blooming across the street. In summer, I sit on the front stoop, a glass of lemonade in my hand as I chat with neighbors. Autumn inspires an arrangement of pumpkins and squash in a display beside my front door. And winter sometimes finds me wrapped in a throw on the porch, listening to the rain.

The seasons show me that nothing lasts forever—that winter, as dark and cold and rainy as it may be, is always followed by spring, a season of light and hope. Though the seasons may change, God's faithfulness is sure and certain, unfailing throughout the seasons of the year and the seasons of my life.

To every thing there is a season, and a time to every purpose under the heaven.

ECCLESIASTES 3:1 KJV

———⁓———

I know, O God, that only
You are forever.
All my trials and joys will
one day be redeemed
by You in eternity.

Amen.

The Gateway to Gratitude

I have a little ritual I carry out each day as I leave for work. I stand on my front porch with my key in the door lock and thank God for my home and all the blessings of this life. It's a small but powerful routine. Gratitude to God prepares me to meet and cope with whatever the day may bring.

God is the giver of all good gifts. He pours out His love, grace, and blessing on me each day. He provides a roof over my head and a lovely front garden. He gives me more than I could ask for, and He does it so quietly that sometimes I barely notice. "And thank You for my front porch," I whisper as I turn to go.

*O give thanks to the L*ORD*, for He is good;*
For His lovingkindness is everlasting.

1 CHRONICLES 16:34 NAS

—᎒w—

O God, remind me to be grateful
for all good things
today and throughout
eternity.
Amen.

Finding Heaven on My Front Porch

I sit on my front porch and watch the world go by. A neighbor drives by on his way to run an errand. Three children ride their bikes up the hill. A mother pushes a stroller along the sidewalk. I notice a couple of neighborhood cats are on the prowl in the garden across the street. Nothing happens. And everything happens.

As I sit here on my front porch, I thank God for the ordinary things and everyday people He has placed in my life. I bask in the warmth of His love and mercy. He has placed a little bit of Heaven right here before my eyes on my own front porch. I am awed. I am grateful. I am at peace.

As you go, preach this message:
"The kingdom of heaven is near."

MATTHEW 10:7 NIV

———ຓ———

God, help me not to miss the little bit
of Heaven You have placed right under
my nose. I want to see Your glory.

Amen.

Entertaining Angels Unaware

A year after my mother died, my seventy-year-old father brought his girlfriend to my house to meet me. I knew Dad had been grief stricken and lonely after my mother passed away. I had hoped that he would meet someone nice—someday. But suddenly, someday was now.

Answering a knock at the door, I found the girlfriend standing on my front porch with my father. My father beamed as he introduced Lynette, who appeared to be in her sixties.

My father married his girlfriend. And I soon came to think of Lynette as an angel sent from Heaven. God's love conquers loneliness, grief, fear, and suspicion. An angel named Lynette told me so.

Do not neglect to show hospitality to strangers, for by this some have entertained angels without knowing it.

HEBREWS 13:2 NAS

～m～

God, give me the courage to entertain angels.
Help me to hear the message they bring to me from You.

Amen.

Listening to a Whisper

It's a couple of hours before dawn. I'm bundled up in a sweater with a lap blanket thrown over my shoulders, sitting on the step of my front porch. It's been a busy week. Lots of meetings. Lots of telephone calls. Lots of conversations with colleagues, friends, and family. Lots of useless chatter. I feel spent.

I've decided to sit here and listen for God's voice. I think He has been whispering in my ear all week, but I haven't been quiet long enough to listen. "Speak to me," I pray. "I'm anxious to hear Your voice." I sit back and close my eyes as I wait for His still, small voice. "Thank You, God, for the stillness of the night and my front-porch sanctuary."

Now a word was brought stealthily,
And my ear received a whisper of it.

JOB 4:12 NAS

God, help me escape the clamor of daily life.
Give me the patience I need to be quiet
and wait to hear Your whisper.

Amen.

Don't Just Sit There—
Do Nothing

Recently I was driving down the street, following one of those large sport-utility vehicles. Through the rear window, I could see that a young woman was driving. She had a cell phone plastered to one ear and seemed to be having an angry conversation with someone. In the backseat were three kids, all of whom seemed to be under the age of ten. The kids were hitting each other. I could only imagine what the decibel level must have been like inside.

As I walked up the steps and sat down in my front-porch rocker, I prayed for the young woman. I asked God to help her find some "time" away from her busy schedule to think, to pray, to listen, to renew herself. In the midst of the errands, the phone calls, and the children, I prayed that God will help her find a few moments to sit on her front porch and do nothing.

The fruit of righteousness
will be peace; the effect
of righteousness will be
quietness and confidence forever.

ISAIAH 32:17 NIV

———✲———

This time of doing nothing, O God, I dedicate
to You. For in Your righteousness
is peace and quietness.

Amen.

The Stars Tell a Story

A few evenings ago, a power outage left me with
no way to entertain myself. No lights to read by.
No TV to watch. No radio or CD player to listen to.
No computer to surf the Internet. The phone was
the only appliance still working, but it was too late
to call anyone. I wasn't ready to go to bed.

"Go outside," said a small voice deep inside. So I
headed for my front-porch sanctuary. Usually, the
lights of the city drown out the stars, but that
night was different. The sky was on fire with
starlight. I stood on my front porch, stunned by
the beauty all around me. What other entertain-
ment could compare with God's own spectacular
light show?

The heavens declare the glory of God;
and the firmament sheweth
his handywork.

PSALM 19:1 KJV

The stars tell Your story, O God.
I give You praise and glory for
Your greatness.

Amen.

God Is in the Details

Lately, I've been giving my house a much-needed face-lift. Whenever I call him, my father appears on my front porch with his tool kit, ready to help with a repair or decorating project. I love my home but couldn't manage it without his help, even when I'm not redecorating. Dad never complains—just a little good-natured grumbling now and then.

Such everyday acts of kindness and generosity are blessings from God—miracles, if you will. As far as I'm concerned, my father is one of God's miracles. Every time I see him standing patiently on my front porch waiting to help me, I know God has richly blessed me.

*I do not cease to give thanks
for you as I remember you
in my prayers.*

EPHESIANS 1:16 NRSV

———ﾧ———

God, help me to recognize the blessings of
kindness and generosity You send my way.

Amen.

The Glory of Thunder

This past autumn, the entire San Francisco Bay area was treated to a spectacular thunder and lightning display. I was at home when I heard the first rumble of thunder late one afternoon. At first I thought it was just a truck driving by. But then I saw the flash and heard an enormous clap of thunder right over my house. For the next hour and a half, I sat on my front porch, watching and listening.

Awe and wonder are spiritual experiences. They keep me from underestimating my Creator and taking our relationship for granted. The magnificence of the thunder and lightning remind me that Someone else is in control of the universe and my life.

Listen closely to the
thunder of His voice,
And the rumbling that goes out
from His mouth.

JOB 37:2 NAS

God, You are the Creator
and I am Your creature.
As I listen to the thunder and see the
lightning, I am filled
with wonder and amazement.
You are truly great!
Amen.

It's All Good

Sometimes I sit on my front porch and just look at my garden. If I'm not careful, I end up watching my garden for hours and neglecting all my chores. My garden is beautiful. It is filled with California native, drought-tolerant plants, mostly flowering shrubs. It is known as an "urban habitat." Most of the plants attract bees, butterflies, and hummingbirds. No fewer than six species of bees feed on my garden flowers.

To me, my garden symbolizes the goodness of God poured out in His creation. It's good for me to remember that when He finished creating the world, He declared it good. When I feel discouraged or overwhelmed, I look at my garden—and drink in the goodness of God.

God saw every thing
that he had made, and,
behold, it was very good.
And the evening and the
morning were the sixth day.

GENESIS 1:31 KJV

God, help me to find
goodness in Your world,
and let me rejoice and celebrate in it.

Amen.

The Wintry Soul

Even California winters limit the time I can spend outside on my front porch. The days are short, and the nights are cold. The rains come, and sometimes they continue for days at a time. When it isn't raining, fog and gray skies often block the sun.

During the winter, it's easy to start feeling discouraged. Even looking out the front window at my garden is depressing—the flowers are gone and the plants are asleep. I can feel winter creeping into my soul.

That is when I most need to remember summer on my front porch—warm and relaxed, watching the flowers grow. Under the eye of our unchanging God, everything has its season.

It was you who set all the boundaries of the earth; you made both summer and winter.

PSALM 74:17 NIV

—⁂—

God, I know that nothing lasts forever, that all things change except You. Give me hope to live through this winter in my soul, that I may rejoice once again when spring comes.

Amen.

Baptized with Rain

Once in a rare while, Oakland gets a late spring rain. Billowy clouds breeze over the city, and soon a gentle rain begins to fall. When this happens, I drop everything I'm doing and head for my front porch. I sit and watch the rain and breathe in the delicious scent of my thirsty garden. The drip and gurgle of rain in the gutters is music to my ears.

When it rains like this, it seems like God is baptizing the world. Most of California, including Oakland, would be a desert without man-made irrigation. So to me, the spring rain is a sign of God's grace showered over a world thirsty for love and mercy. I rock in my rocking chair, grateful to be aware of this moment of grace.

In the light of the king's countenance is life; and his favour is as a cloud of the latter rain.

PROVERBS 16:15 KJV

———

Let me not miss those moments of grace You send, O God. Help me to recognize them, so I may give You thanks.
Amen

The Meaning of Rest

During the summer, I set up a hammock on my front porch. As much as I enjoy resting in it on a warm summer's day, I always feel a certain sense of guilt. *Surely*, I think as I lie there enjoying the day, *I should be doing something constructive.*

Unfortunately, I feel twinges of that same guilt with regard to God. Too often I feel uncomfortable just resting in God. I keep thinking I should be working harder—attending more church services, visiting more shut-ins, serving on more committees, praying more, studying the Bible more, etc. I'm learning, though, that it is deeply beneficial just to rest in the arms of God, to let Him renew my strength so that I can continue to show His kindness to others.

Take my yoke upon you
and learn from me,
for I am gentle and
humble in heart,
and you will find rest
for your souls.

MATTHEW 11:29 NIV

God, in You let
me find rest for my
soul today.
Amen.

A Place to Cool Off

My dad had been helping me with some minor repairs. We'd been working all morning with hardly a break. We were getting tired, hungry, and cranky. Soon, we found ourselves disagreeing about the best way to patch a hole in the laundry-room wall. I suggested we take a break and headed to the front porch to cool off.

"I'm only human, Lord," I prayed testily, while rocking furiously in the rocking chair, "so give me a break!" I rocked and rocked until finally my anger began to subside. Patching a hole in the wall of a room where I kept nothing but my dirty clothes didn't seem like such a big deal after all. "Thank you, God," I prayed quietly as I went to fix Dad's lunch.

A fool gives full vent to anger,
but the wise quietly holds it back.

PROVERBS 29:11 NRSV

———m———

O God, sometimes I get so angry
I can't see straight. Help me
to cool down.
Give me Your perspective.
Amen.

Gentle, Gentle Time

For me, the best time of the day is dawn. I don't mind sacrificing a little extra sleep to get up early, sit on my front porch, and quietly await this gentle miracle—the sun coming up on another day. Not many people share my passion for dawn. I'm the only one up and about on my street. Only the birds are awake, singing in anticipation of the new day.

God seems nearer to me at dawn than at any other time of the day. During those moments before the sun rises, I can almost feel His gentle touch. Light rapidly fills the sky. The sun itself peeks over the horizon. Another day is born. And I am, once again, awed by God's gentle power.

*Let your gentle spirit be known
to all men. The Lord is near.*

PHILIPPIANS 4:5 NAS

———

Let me know Your gentleness,
O God, and the light touch
of Your presence.

Amen.

A Place to Talk

One autumn, Laura, my best friend from college, came to visit for a few days. As we greeted each other, my mind went back twenty years to Laura's wedding. She and John seemed to be the perfect couple—they loved God and each other very much. Because of their faith, I was certain their marriage would last forever. But I was wrong. Laura and John were divorcing.

Laura and I sat on the front porch while she told me how her marriage had failed. God gave me the words I needed to encourage and strengthen my friend—words of hope that her faith would be renewed and words of promise that she would develop a sweetness of soul.

Pleasant words are like a honeycomb,
sweetness to the soul and health to the body.

PROVERBS 16:24 NRSV

—⁓—

O God, sometimes human love doesn't turn out the
way it should. Let me hear pleasant words that
can restore to me sweetness in my soul.

Amen.

The Spirit's Breath

Sometimes God seems far away. No matter how many prayers I pray, Bible passages I read, or church services I attend, I can't seem to sense His presence. During those "far away" times, I wait quietly on my front porch, listening for His voice. Sometimes I must wait a long time.

But if I am patient enough and attentive enough, I begin to feel the peace that accompanies His presence. Joy begins to bubble up within me until the tears are flowing and I am caught up in His glory once again. I know that God never leaves me. He has promised to abide with me forever, but sometimes my receiver needs to be adjusted. My heart needs to be tuned again to the voice of the Creator.

You will show me the path of life;
In Your presence is fullness of joy;
At Your right hand are pleasures forevermore.

PSALM 16:11 NKJV

—⚬—

Sometimes You seem
so far away, O God.
Let me feel the breath of
Your Spirit once again.
Amen.

Pay Attention

The world is such a big place these days. The area where I live is enjoying lots of newfound wealth. Big homes, big sport-utility vehicles, big luxury boats—all purchased with big money.

Now I have nothing against being big. My house, which I love dearly, is big. But I must remember that big isn't always better. God has created a world full of big things—mountains, the star-filled heavens, and the crashing waves of the sea, to name a few. But He has also placed His signature on the small things—the eyes of a loved one, the purring of a cat, the beauty of a rose, the dawn's quiet on my front porch. I will remember to look for God's handiwork in all His creation—the big and the small!

Since the creation of the world His invisible attributes are clearly seen, being understood by the things that are made, even His eternal power and Godhead.

ROMANS 1:20 NKJV

—〰—

O God, let me find You today in the small things right under my nose.

Amen.

The Soul's Entrance

Real estate in California is expensive, and good homes are difficult to find. I was outbid five times before finding the house where I now live. There were already four bids on this property when I found it. In order to secure the contract, I had to offer many thousands of dollars more than the asking price. When I stood on the front porch of my new home for the first time as owner, I knew it was worth every penny.

The life of faith is not easy either. It's difficult to believe in God's mercy when I see all the suffering in the world. But God calls me to believe in His mercy, love, and forgiveness in spite of life's ambiguities. A life of faith is not easy, but it's well worth the investment.

Strive to enter through the narrow door; for many, I tell you, will seek to enter and will not be able.

LUKE 13:24 NAS

O God, give me the courage to enter by the narrow door, trusting in You and only in You. *Amen*.

Believing Is Seeing

Not long ago, I had a sudden urge to clean. No corner was safe from my dust rag, mop, broom, or arsenal of cleaners. I scrubbed, scoured, and wiped down every inch of every surface inside my house. Then I moved outside to the front porch. Cobwebs had gathered around the front door and above me on the ceiling.

I had just raised my broom to sweep the ceiling when I noticed the most perfect web with a large beautiful spider sitting in the middle. The magnificent web with its lone occupant made an unusual but fitting tribute to the beauty and endless variety of God's creation. I leaned my broom against the wall, sat down in my rocker, and watched.

There are four things which are little on the earth, but they are exceedingly wise…
The spider skillfully grasps with its hands, and it is in kings' palaces.

PROVERBS 30:24,28 NKJV

Don't let me overlook You today, God.
Help me to really see Your
handiwork all around me.

Amen.

A Point of Departure

"I love you, baby," my mother said to me over the phone. The next day, I learned she had died. Her death was sudden, unexpected, and a horrible shock. After three years, I am still working through my grief. I am now more aware than ever that death is a reality for human beings. That's why we must strive to show love and appreciation for one another each and every day.

When guests leave my house, I stand on the front porch to see them off in the same way I welcomed them only hours before—with love. I wave good-bye as they leave and pray for their safe arrival home. And I pray that we will one day soon meet again.

Be very careful, then, how you live—
not as unwise but as wise, making
the most of every opportunity.

EPHESIANS 5:15-16 NIV

—◆◆◆—

God, keep each guest that leaves
my house in the palm of Your
hand. And may we know many
more merry meetings.

Amen.

Give Me Shelter

As I sit here under the shelter of my front porch, it's easy to remember the many times that God has delivered me from trouble. When I was unemployed, He helped me find a job. When I was sick, He helped me find health and wholeness. When I was depressed, He helped me find joy and renewed hope. He has been a shelter to me.

I look up at the blue, blue sky and thank God for keeping me in the day of trouble. When I need Him, He is always there, ready to help. How wonderful it is to be kept by His love and grace.

*In the day of trouble he
will keep me safe in his
dwelling; he will hide me in the
shelter of his tabernacle and set
me high upon a rock.*

PSALM 27:5 NIV

—✍—

O God, You are my Savior and my deliverer in
all things without and all things within.
All glory and thanks to You, O God.

Amen.

All Shall Be Well

One of my favorite sayings comes from Julian of Norwich, a great Christian philosopher from many centuries ago—"And all shall be well, and all manner of thing shall be well."

All is well from my front porch. My beautiful garden, my community of neighbors and friends, the glorious California sky, and the birds in full song declare that all is well. No matter what the future holds, God's grace will be enough to ensure that all is well with my soul. Tough times? If they should come my way, they will find me sitting on my front porch, proclaiming that God is good and all is well indeed.

Beloved, I pray that all may go well with you
and that you may be in good health,
just as it is well with your soul.

3 John 2 NRSV

O God, with and in You all is well. Grant that
all will be well with my soul today.
Amen.

For a Thousand Tongues to Sing

My grandparents' screened porch is a common element in many of my earliest memories. On hot summer evenings, Granny would lead me outside and hold me in her lap. We would sit there singing softly in the dark, humid air, "This little light of mine, I'm gonna let it shine." Sometimes a thunderstorm would pass through, but I was never afraid. As long as Granny held me and we sang about God, I felt safe.

Even today you can find me sitting outside on warm summer evenings, softly singing, "Let it shine, let it shine, let it shine." I am grateful for God's love. We don't really need "a thousand tongues to sing," just a warm summer's evening, a welcoming porch, and a simple song.

O sing to the LORD a new song,
for he has done marvelous things.

PSALM 98:1 NRSV

Thank You, God, for Your love that holds
me in the palm of Your hand.
Amen.

This, Too, Shall Pass

The front porch is a wonderful place to sit and watch what is going on in the neighborhood. From my porch, I've learned that nothing stays the same. The neighbors across the street replaced their lawn with a large garden. The house on the corner has a new owner, and the kid who delivered my newspaper for five years starts college this fall.

My front porch teaches me that all things change and pass away over time. Both good times and bad times pass away. Only God never changes. I must set my mind on God's things that are above because the things on this earth change constantly. Only God stays unfailingly the same over the course of time.

*The mind set on the Spirit
is life and peace.*

ROMANS 8:6 NAS

—☙—

God, help me to trust You in spite of all
the change that swirls about me. I know
I can count on Your unchanging love.

Amen.

Wonder in an Ant Trail

The kingdom of God can be found in the strangest of places. Recently, I sat down to rest on the stoop of my front porch. Soon I noticed an ant trail winding its way from one side of the sidewalk to the other. The ants marched along, totally focused on their destination. Some ants carried little burdens, while others ran to and fro along the trail tending to other "ant" business.

As I watched them march along, I marveled at God's creative genius. Each creature has been invested with what it needs to survive and thrive. We are the most unique of all God's creatures, for we are created in His own likeness. I know that as I trust Him, He will provide all I need to survive and thrive in this life.

My God will fully supply every need of yours according to his riches in glory in Christ Jesus.

PHILIPPIANS 4:19 NRSV

—⁂—

God, You give me all I need to live for today. Thank You for Your love and provision.
Amen.

My Front-Porch Sanctuary

My front porch is my sanctuary. I go there to get away from telephones, e-mail, family demands, and pressures from work. As I sit in my front-porch sanctuary and watch the world go by, trouble and stress melt away for a little while. After a tough day, I need my front-porch sanctuary more than ever.

Everyone needs a sanctuary in which to find rest and renewal. A front porch can be a place where we leave our troubles behind for a while, gain perspective about our lives, and come to a greater understanding of God's love for us and for the world around us.

One thing I asked of the LORD, that
will I seek after: to live in the house of the
LORD all the days of my life, to behold the beauty
of the LORD, and to inquire in his temple.

PSALM 27:4 NRSV

—〰—

God, my front porch has become my sanctuary.
Cover me with Your mercy as I rest here and
look out over my world.

Amen.

Discovering the Forgotten Room

According to many architects, the American front porch is being rediscovered. More and more people are looking for homes that connect them to their neighbors and give them a sense of a slower, simpler time. The traditional front porch has become a symbol of that search for community and simple down-home values.

There is also a spiritual lesson to be learned. A front porch provides an opportunity to slow down long enough to reconnect with God by spending time in quiet reflection. It can serve as a sanctuary for those who take the time to appreciate its unique window on the world.

Be transformed by the renewing of your minds, so that you may discern what is the will of God—what is good and acceptable and perfect.

ROMANS 12:2 NRSV

—⚬—

God, let me meet You on my heart's front porch
during this busy day. For to do
Your will, O Lord, is the
delight of my heart.

Amen.